A
Rookie
reader®

Jenny's Socks

Written by Carol Murray
Illustrated by Priscilla Burris

Children's Press®
A Division of Scholastic Inc.
New York • Toronto • London • Auckland • Sydney
Mexico City • New Delhi • Hong Kong
Danbury, Connecticut

To my mom, Dorothy from Kansas,
who washed my socks for many years.
—C.M.

For Ellen Sussman, from a grateful heart
—P.B.

Reading Consultants

Linda Cornwell
Literacy Specialist

Katharine A. Kane
Education Consultant
(Retired, San Diego County Office of Education and San Diego State University)

Library of Congress Cataloging-in-Publication Data
Murray, Carol.
  Jenny's socks / written by Carol Murray ; illustrated by Priscilla
Burris.
      p. cm. – (A rookie reader)
Summary: Jenny has beautiful socks in lots of colors, but her favorite
is her pet cat Socks.
  ISBN 0-516-25899-0 (lib. bdg.)   0-516-26826-0 (pbk.)
  [1. Socks–Fiction. 2. Cats–Fiction. 3. Stories in rhyme.] I. Burris,
Priscilla, ill. II. Title. III. Series.
  PZ8.3.M936Je 2003
  [E]-dc21

                              2003007121

CHILDREN'S PRESS, and A ROOKIE READER®, and associated logos are trademarks
and or registered trademarks of Scholastic Library Publishing. SCHOLASTIC and
associated logos are trademarks and or registered trademarks of Scholastic Inc.
5 6 7 8 9 10 R 13 12 11 10 09   62

Some of Jenny's socks are green.

The prettiest green you've ever seen.

Some of Jenny's socks are blue.

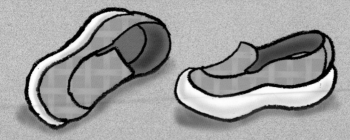

Blue as the ocean. Silver blue.

Most of Jenny's socks are white.
Soft and cozy. Shiny bright.

Thin or heavy.

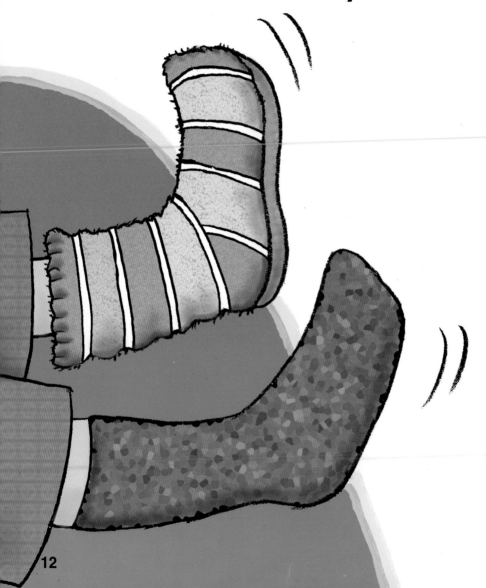

Loose or tight.

Long or short.
They are all just right.

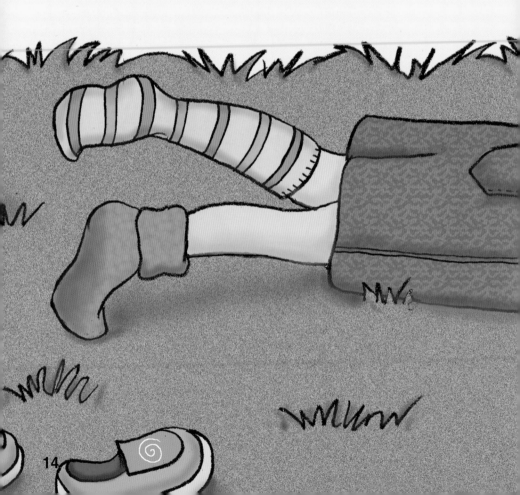

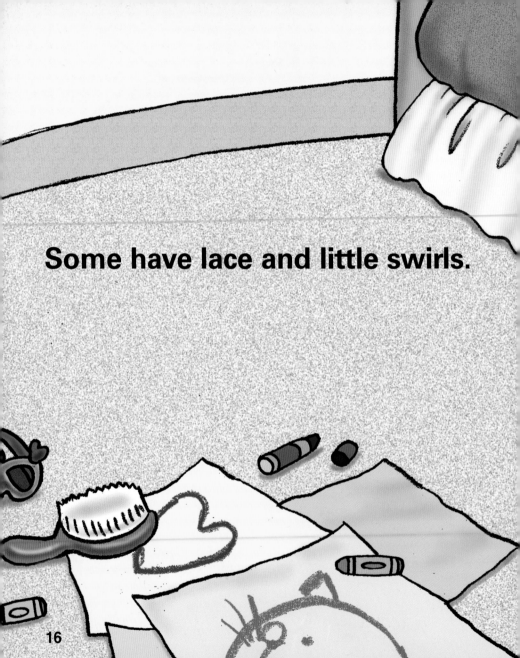

Some have lace and little swirls.

Fancy socks for fancy girls.

Some are red and white and blue.

They say, "America, we love you!"

Some have stars, and some have bears.

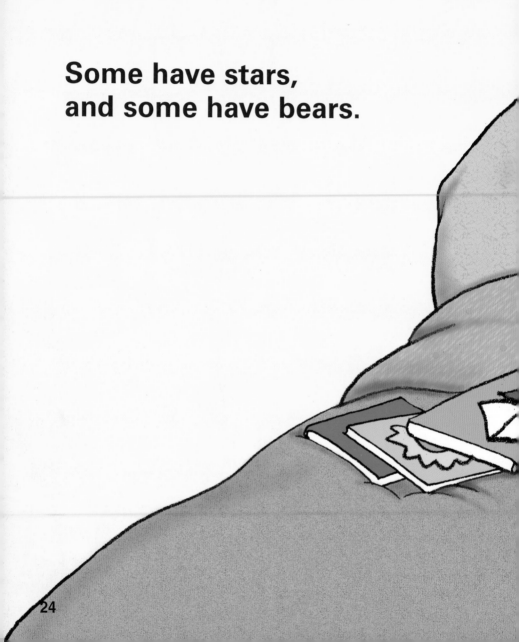

There are many other pairs.

Just look into this little box.

You'll find Jenny's favorite Socks.

Word List (59 words)

all	girls	ocean	some
America	green	of	stars
and	have	or	swirls
are	heavy	other	the
as	into	pairs	there
bears	Jenny's	prettiest	they
blue	just	red	thin
box	lace	right	this
bright	little	say	tight
cozy	long	seen	we
ever	look	shiny	white
fancy	loose	short	you
favorite	love	silver	you'll
find	many	socks	you've
for	most	soft	

About the Author

Carol Murray is a teacher and a published poet. She taught English and Speech at Hutchinson Community College for twenty-five years. She lives in the country in Kansas with her husband, Max, and two quarter horses named Lucky and Bud. Her favorite animal is the giraffe. She especially likes kids and poetry and black and white cats.

About the Illustrator

Priscilla Burris has illustrated numerous books for children; one of which she is also the author. She loves silly socks, books, drawing, and being with her family. Priscilla lives happily in Southern California with her husband, Craig, their three children, ages 13, 14, and 18, and Casper their friendly dog.